WRECK THIS JOURNAL

TO CREATE IS TO DESTROY

BY KERI SMITH

PENGUIN
BOOKS

PENGUIN BOOKS

UK ı USA ı CANADA ı IRELAND ı AUSTRALIA
INDIA ı NEW ZEALAND ı SOUTH AFRICA

PENGUIN BOOKS IS PART OF THE PENGUIN RANDOM HOUSE GROUP OF COMPANIES
WHOSE ADDRESSES CAN BE FOUND AT GLOBAL.PENGUINRANDOMHOUSE.COM.

FIRST PUBLISHED IN THE UNITED STATES OF AMERICA BY PENGUIN GROUP (USA) INC., 2007
FIRST PUBLISHED IN GREAT BRITAIN BY PENGUIN BOOKS 2010
THIS EXPANDED EDITION PUBLISHED 2013
036

PRINTED IN GREAT BRITAIN BY CLAYS LTD, ELCOGRAF S.P.A.

978-0-141-97614-3

www.greenpenguin.co.uk

MIX
Paper from
responsible sources
FSC™ C018179

Penguin Books is committed to a sustainable
future for our business, our readers and our planet.
This book is made from Forest Stewardship
Council™ certified paper.

WARNING: DURING THE PROCESS OF THIS BOOK YOU WILL GET DIRTY. YOU MAY FIND YOURSELF COVERED IN PAINT, OR ANY OTHER NUMBER OF FOREIGN SUBSTANCES. YOU WILL GET WET. YOU MAY BE ASKED TO DO THINGS YOU QUESTION. YOU MAY GRIEVE FOR THE PERFECT STATE THAT YOU FOUND THE BOOK IN. YOU MAY BEGIN TO SEE CREATIVE DESTRUCTION EVERYWHERE. YOU MAY BEGIN TO LIVE MORE RECKLESSLY.

Acknowledgments This book was made with the help of the following people: my husband, Jefferson Pitcher, who provides constant inspiration for living a full and daring life (some of his ideas ended up here). Thanks to the talented artists Steve Lambert and Cynthia Yardley-Lambert who helped me brainstorm ideas during a lecture on contemporary art. To my editor at Perigee, Meg Leder, who embraced and believed in this project from the beginning, your thoughts and sensitivity left me with so much gratitude. To my agent, Faith Hamlin, for continuing to believe in my artistic/creative vision. Thanks also to Corita Kent, John Cage, Ross Mendes, Brenda Ueland, Bruno Munari, and Charles and Rae Eames, whose ideas and perceptions continue to rip me wide open.
Dedicated to perfectionists all over the world.

THIS BOOK BELONGS TO:

_____

WRITE YOUR NAME IN WHITE.

_____

WRITE YOUR NAME ILLEGIBLY.

_____

WRITE YOUR NAME IN TINY LETTERS.

_____

WRITE YOUR NAME BACKWARD.

_____

WRITE YOUR NAME VERY FAINTLY.

_____

WRITE YOUR NAME USING LARGE LETTERS.

_____

ADDRESS

_____

PHONE NUMBER

* NOTE: IF FOUND, FLIP TO A PAGE RANDOMLY,
         FOLLOW THE INSTRUCTIONS, THEN RETURN.

1. Carry this with you everywhere you go.
2. Follow the instructions on every page.
3. Order is not important.
4. Instructions are open to interpretation.
5. Experiment.
(work against your better judgment.)

materials

ideas
gum
glue
dirt
saliva
water
weather
garbage
plant life
pencil/pen
needle & thread
stamps
stickers
sticky things
sticks
spoons
comb
twist tie
ink
paint
grass
detergent
grease
tears
crayons

smells
hands
string
ball
unpredictability
spontaneity
photos
newspaper
white things
office supplies
wax
found items
stapler
food
tea/coffee
emotions
fears
shoes
matches
biology
scissors
tape
time
happenstance
gumption
sharp things

ADD YOUR OWN PAGE NUMBERS.

STARTING HERE

CRACK THE SPINE.

LEAVE THIS PAGE

BLANK

ON PURPOSE.

STAND HERE.

(WIPE YOUR FEET, JUMP UP AND DOWN.)

POKE HOLES IN THIS PAGE USING A PENCIL.

DRAW FAT LINES AND THIN.

PUSHING REALLY HARD WITH THE PENCIL.

THIS PAGE IS FOR HANDPRINTS
OR FINGERPRINTS.
GET THEM DIRTY THEN PRESS DOWN.

COLOR THIS ENTIRE PAGE.

50

25

10

5

0

THROW SOMETHING

A PENCIL, A BALL DIPPED IN PAINT.

PRESS LEAVES AND OTHER FOUND THINGS

SCRATCH

USING A SHARP OBJECT.

DO SOME RUBBINGS WITH A PENCIL.

SCRIBBLE WILDLY, VIOLENTLY, *with* RECKLESS ABANDON.

TEAR STRIPS
RIP IT UP!

GLUE, staple, OR tape these PAGES together.

draw lines
ON THE BUS, ON A

While IN MOTION.
TRAIN, WHILE WALKING.

FILL THIS PAGE WITH CIRCLES.

Document your dinner.

RUB, SMEAR, SPLATTER YOUR FOOD.

USE THIS PAGE AS A NAPKIN.

CHEW ON this.

↓

*WARNING: DO NOT SWALLOW.

MAKE A FUNNEL.

DRINK SOME WATER.

1. CUT
   OUT.

2. ROLL
   & TAPE.

3. ADD WATER
   & DRINK.

(TEAR OUT)

CRUMPLE.

MAKE A PAPER AIRPLANE.

like this

WRAP something

WITH THIS PAGE.

TONGUE PAINTING

1. EAT SOME COLORFUL CANDY.

2. LICK THIS PAGE.

WRITE ONE WORD

OVER AND OVER.

TIE A STRING TO THE *spine* OF THIS BOOK.

SWING WILDLY

LET IT HIT THE WALLS.

PICK UP THE JOURNAL WITHOUT USING YOUR HANDS.

compost this page.

watch it deteriorate.

DO A *really* UGLY
(USE UGLY SUBJECT MATTER:
A BADLY DRAWN BIRD,

DRAWING

GUM, POO, DEAD THINGS,
MOLD, BARF, CRUD.)

PRETEND YOU
ARE DOODLING
ON THE BACK
OF AN ENVEL-
OPE WHILE
ON THE PHONE.

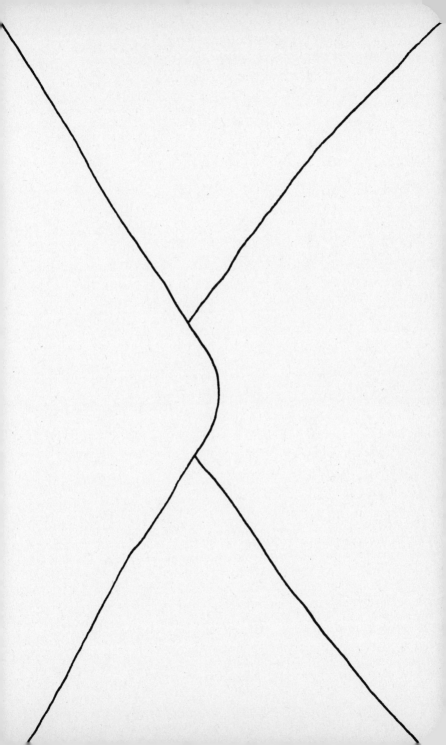

JOURNAL GOLF

1. TEAR OUT PAGE. CRUMPLE INTO A BALL.

2. PLACE JOURNAL INTO A TRIANGLE SHAPE.

3. HIT/KICK THE BALL THROUGH THE TRIANGLE.

make a paper chain.

COLLECT FRUIT STICKERS* HERE.

* STICKERS YOU FIND ON BOUGHT FRUIT.

COVER THIS PAGE

USING ONLY office SUPPLIES.

BRING THIS BOOK IN THE SHOWER WITH YOU.

GO FOR A WALK, DRAG IT.

TIE A STRING TO THE JOURNAL.

USE THIS AS A

test Page

FOR PENS, PAINTS,
MARKERS, OR ART SUPPLIES.

DRIP
SOMETHING
HERE.
(INK, PAINT, TEA)
CLOSE THE BOOK
TO MAKE A
PRINT.

Sew this page

glue A RANDOM PAGE FROM A NEWSPAPER HERE.

A PLACE FOR YOUR GROCERY LISTS.

COLLECT THE STAMPS OFF OF ALL YOUR MAIL.

TRACE THE THINGS IN YOUR BAG (OR POCKETS). LET THE LINES OVERLAP.

COVER THIS PAGE

WITH WHITE THINGS.

scribble wildly using only borrowed pens.
(document where they were borrowed from.)

MAKE A SUDDEN, DESTRUCTIVE, UNPREDICTABLE MOVEMENT WITH THE JOURNAL.

MAKE A MESS,
CLEAN IT UP.

DOODLE OVER TOP OF:

- ☐ THE COVER.
- ☐ THE TITLE PAGE.
- ☐ THE INSTRUCTIONS.
- ☐ THE COPYRIGHT PAGE.

FOLD DOWN THE CORNERS
OF YOUR FAVORITE PAGES.

Page of good thoughts.

MAKE PRINTS USING AN INK PAD AND CUT VEGETABLES.

ASK A FRIEND
TO DO SOMETHING
DESTRUCTIVE
TO THIS PAGE.
DON'T LOOK.

WRITE CARELESSLY.
NOW.

GLUE RANDOM ITEMS HERE.
(i.e., things you find in your couch, on the street, etc.)

tear this page out.

PUT IT IN YOUR POCKET.
PUT IT THROUGH THE WASH.
STICK IT BACK IN.

CUT THROUGH SEVERAL LAYERS

Infuse this page with a smell of your choosing.

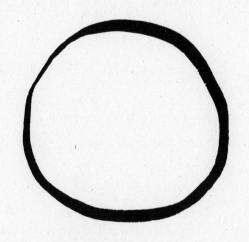

COLOR OUTSIDE
OF THE LINES.

CLOSE YOUR EYES.

CONNECT THE DOTS
FROM MEMORY.

HANG THE JOURNAL IN A PUBLIC PLACE.
INVITE PEOPLE TO DRAW HERE.

COLLECT YOUR

GLUE IT HERE.

↙ ↓ ↓ ↘

POCKET LINT.

trace YOUR hand.

SAMPLE VARIOUS SUBSTANCES FOUND IN YOUR HOME.

DOCUMENT WHAT THEY ARE.
CREATE COLOR THEMES.

DOCUMENT A BORING

EVENT IN DETAIL.

CREATE A DRAWING USING A PIECE (OR SEVERAL PIECES) OF YOUR HAIR.

```
┌ ─ ─ ─ ─ ─ ─ ─ ─ ─ ─ ─ ─ ┐
│                         │
│                         │
│                         │
│       STICK PHOTO       │
│         HERE.           │
│                         │
│                         │
│                         │
│                         │
│                         │
└ ─ ─ ─ ─ ─ ─ ─ ─ ─ ─ ─ ─ ┘
```

glue in a photo of
yourself you dislike.

DEFACE.

DRAW LINES USING
WRITING UTENSILS
(STICKS, SPOONS, TWIST TIES,

fill in this
page when
you are really
ANGRY.

WRITE OR DRAW

WITH YOUR LEFT HAND.

FIND A
WAY TO
WEAR THE
JOURNAL.

this page is a sign.
what do you want it to say?

CREATE A NONSTOP LINE.

SPACE FOR NEGATIVE COMMENTS.*

(* WHAT IS YOUR INNER CRITIC SAYING?)

DRAW LINES WITH YOUR PEN OR PENCIL.

LICK YOUR FINGER AND SMEAR THE LINES.

LOSE THIS PAGE.

(THROW IT OUT.)

ACCEPT THE LOSS.

A PAGE for FOUR-LETTER WORDS.

GLUE IN A PAGE FROM A MAGAZINE.

CIRCLE WORDS YOU LIKE.

write with the pen in your mouth.

GIVE AWAY YOUR FAVORITE PAGE.

Write backwards.

THIS SPACE IS DEDICATED

TO INTERNAL MONOLOGUE.

SCRUB THIS PAGE.

HIDE A SECRET MESSAGE SOMEWHERE IN THIS BOOK.

SLEEP WITH THE JOURNAL.

(Describe the experience here.)

CLOSE THE JOURNAL.

WRITE/SCRIBBLE SOMETHING ON THE EDGES.

WRITE A LIST OF MORE WAYS TO
WRECK THIS JOURNAL.

1.

2.

3.

4.

5.

6.

7.

8.

9.

10.

11.

12.

STAIN LOG

DOODLE OVER TOP OF THIS PAGE ↓↓↓ AND IN THE MARGINS.

This is not an important piece of writing. The author of this work is writing with the intention of creating a body of text that has little or no meaning. It is merely a texture of sorts that the reader will view as a canvas. Hopefully it will simulate a book that is embedded in your memory, a book you had in your childhood, the one that you secretly wrote in with your crayons. Maybe you were scolded for this by someone.

It could be your first textbook, which you defaced with your pen, prompted by the previous owner's little scrawlings. It was not your fault. Textbooks are destined to be defaced, it is a part of their nature. You are not to be blamed. Anything as boring as a textbook deserves everything it gets.

Are you reading this? You are supposed to be defacing this page. Please stop reading at once! This is your chance to deface something.

Maybe it is not as alluring because you are being told to do it. In that case I command you to cease your drawing immediately! If you make one more mark on this page the author will personally ban you from reading any future books of hers, in perpetuity (or for as long as she continues to make books, which will probably be for a very long time).

There are many things that you could do in place of defacing this page that would be more benefi-cial. Some examples include going to the dentist, cleaning out your fridge, washing the windows, cleaning under your bed, reading the entire works of Proust, arranging your food alphabetically, conducting a scientific study of polymer synthesis and its effects on the world, arranging your envelopes according to size, counting how many sheets of paper you have in your possession, making sure that all of your socks have partners, documenting your pocket lint (oh, yes you already did that earlier in this book), calling your mother back, learning to speak a new language, recording yourself sleeping, moving your furniture around to simulate a bus station, experimenting with new methods of sitting that you've never tried before, jogging on the spot for an hour, pretending you are a secret agent, decorating the inside of your fridge, drawing a fake door on your wall with chalk, conversing with your animal neighbors, writing a speech for a future award, walking to the corner store as slowly as possible, writing a positive feedback letter to your mail delivery person, putting a secret note into a library book, practicing finger strengthening exercises, dressing up as your favorite author, smelling the inside of your nose, memorizing *The Elements of Style* by Strunk and White, sitting on your front porch with a sign that says "Honk if you love birds," documenting the plants in your life on paper, smelling this book, sleeping, pretending to be a famous astronaut.

FIGURE OUT A WAY
TO [ATT ACH] THESE
TWO PAGES TOGETHER.

RUB THIS PAGE ON A DIRTY CAR.

COLLECT
THE LETTER
"W"
HERE.

X COLLECT
DEAD
BUGS
HERE.

DRUM ON THIS
PAGE WITH PENCILS.

FLOAT THIS PAGE.

FIGURE OUT
A WAY TO
FREEZE
THIS PAGE.

HIDE THIS PAGE IN
YOUR NEIGHBOR'S
YARD.

ROLL THE JOURNAL DOWN A LARGE HILL.

SELL THIS PAGE.

SLIDE THE JOURNAL (THIS PAGE FACE-DOWN), DOWN A LONG HALLWAY.

SMUSH
SOMETHING
COLORFUL
ONTO THIS
PAGE.

SQUIRT LIQUID HERE

(TRY USING YOUR MOUTH).

COVER THIS PAGE IN TAPE

(CREATE SOME KIND OF PATTERN).

TRACE YOUR TOES.

ALSO FROM KERI SMITH

NOW AVAILABLE FOR APPLE, ANDROID, AND NOOK DEVICES!

FOR MORE INFORMATION, VISIT
PENGUIN.COM/KERISMITH • PENGUIN.COM/WRECKTHISAPP

T174.0212